Hamartiology

Understanding Our Sin Problem

Gregory Brown

Publishing

Endorsements

"The Bible Teacher's Guide … will help any teacher study and get a better background for his/her Bible lessons. In addition, it will give direction and scope to teaching of the Word of God. Praise God for this contemporary introduction to the Word of God."

—Dr. Elmer Towns
Co-founder of Liberty University
Former Dean, Liberty Baptist Theological Seminary

"Expositional, theological, and candidly practical! I highly recommend The Bible Teacher's Guide for anyone seeking to better understand or teach God's Word."

—Dr. Young–Gil Kim
Founding President, Handong Global University

"Helpful to both the layman and the serious student, The Bible Teacher's Guide, by Dr. Greg Brown, is outstanding!"

—Dr. Neal Weaver
Chancellor, Louisiana Baptist University

"Whether you are preparing a Bible study, a sermon, or simply wanting to dive deeper into a personal study of God's Word, these will be very helpful tools."

—Eddie Byun
Associate Professor of Christian Ministry, Biola University
Author of Justice Awakening

"I am happy that Greg is making his insights into God's truth available to a wider audience through these books. They bear the hallmarks of good Bible teaching: the result of rigorous Bible study and thoroughgoing application to the lives of people."

—Ajith Fernando
Teaching Director, Youth for Christ
Author of A Call to Joy and Pain

"The content of the series is rich. My prayer is that God will use it to help the body of Christ grow strong."

—Dr. Min Chung
Senior Pastor, Covenant Fellowship Church, Urbana, Illinois
Adjunct Professor, Urbana Theological Seminary

"Knowing the right questions to ask and how to go about answering them is fundamental to learning in any subject matter. Greg demonstrates this convincingly."

—Dr. William Moulder
Professor of Biblical Studies, Trinity International University

"Pastor Greg is passionate about the Word of God, rigorous and thorough in his approach to the study of it... I am pleased to recommend The Bible Teacher's Guide to anyone who hungers for the living Word."

—Dr. JunMo Cho
Professor of Linguistics, Handong Global University
Contemporary Christian Music Recording Artist

"I can't imagine any student of Scripture not benefiting by this work."

—Steven J. Cole
Pastor, Flagstaff Christian Fellowship, Flagstaff, Arizona
Author of the Riches from the Word series

"Greg deals with the principles, doctrines, and applications of the text in a practical way which is useful for both individual growth or for help in preparation for teaching."

—Bob Deffinbaugh
Ministry Coordinator, Bible.org
Founding Pastor, Community Bible Chapel, Richardson, Texas

Content

Preface

And entrust what you heard me say in the presence of many others as witnesses to faithful people who will be competent to teach others as well.
2 Timothy 2:2 (NET)

Paul's words to Timothy still apply to us today. The church needs teachers who clearly and fearlessly teach the Word of God. With this in mind, The Bible Teacher's Guide (BTG) series was created. This series includes both expositional and topical studies, with resources to help teachers lead small groups, pastors prepare sermons, and individuals increase their knowledge of God's Word.

Hamartiology can be used for personal study or as a six to nine-session small group curriculum, depending on how the leader divides up the topics. For small groups, the members will read a chapter (or chapters) and discuss the reflection questions and anything else that stood out in the reading within their gathering. Or, the chapter can be read before the gathering, with the meeting focusing only on discussion.

Introduction

In the Bible, every chapter includes sin and its consequences, except four—the first two chapters of Genesis, before the fall, and the last two of Revelation, after the creation of the new heaven and earth. The story of the Bible essentially abounds with the themes of sin and our need for salvation. Since sin permeates every aspect of the human existence, we must understand it and how God provides grace to deliver us from it, both for ourselves and to help others.

In *Hamartiology*, our sin problem and its remedy are explored by answering questions like: *What is sin? What is sin's origin? Why did God allow sin in the first place? Is every sin equal? What is the unpardonable sin? What is the sin that results in death? What are temptations to sin and consequences of it? How can we conquer sin?* and much more. Let's study these together to find grace and mercy to walk in victory over sin. May God the Father, the Son, and the Holy Spirit richly bless your study!

What Is Sin?

What exactly is sin? Wayne Grudem says, "Sin is any failure to conform to the moral law of God in act, attitude, or nature."[1] Simply, sin is when we fail to look like God and depend on him. Tony Evans said this about sin:

> Sin makes us self-centered and self-dependent instead of God centered and God-dependent. The less you need God, the more sinful you have become, because you are trying to function independently of the Creator.[2]

Though there are eight words used for sin in the Old Testament and twelve in the New Testament, the two primary words used for sin, "chata" (Hebrew) and "hamartia" (Greek), have the same basic meaning which is "to miss the mark."[3] These words were used of someone shooting an arrow and missing the target. What target do people miss when they sin? It is the target of looking like God. Romans 3:23 says, "For all have sinned and fall short of the glory of God." When God made Adam and Eve in the garden, they were made in the very image of God (Gen 1:27). Image doesn't refer to their physical makeup, since God is a spirit and does not have a physical form (John 4:4). Image, at the minimum, refers to humanity's character and function. Adam and Eve were made with a righteous disposition—a desire to honor God and love others. In addition, as a matter of function, they were called to rule the earth, even as God ruled heaven. They were essentially God's vice-regents. Adam and Eve were to display God's image and glory to all of creation, as benevolent stewards. When humans fail to do this in thought, word, or action, we miss the mark. We sin by failing to live according to our original purpose as bearers of God's image.

Another definition of sin is "lawlessness." First John 3:4 says, "Everyone who practices sin also practices lawlessness; indeed, sin is lawlessness." When people break God's laws, which are ultimately summed up in loving God and others (Matt 20:37-40, Gal 5:14), we sin.

Sometimes people categorize sins as sins of commission and sins of omission. A sin of commission is when we "commit" a sin by breaking one of God's prohibitions, such as: do not lie, steal, or covet. A sin of omission is when we "omit" doing something God commands, such as making disciples, going to church, or serving those in need. James 4:17 says, "So whoever knows what is good to do and does not do it is guilty of sin."

Another aspect of sin that is important to remember is that sin is first of all committed in the heart before it is acted out. In Matthew 15:18-20, Christ said:

> But the things that come out of the mouth come from the heart, and these things defile a person. For out of the heart come evil ideas, murder, adultery, sexual immorality, theft, false testimony, slander. These are the things that defile a person; it is not eating with unwashed hands that defiles a person.

Murder, sexual immorality, lies, theft, slander, and every other evil thing first start in the heart. In fact, in Matthew 5, Christ simply taught that if a man lusted after a woman that was not his wife, he had committed adultery (v. 27-28). He also taught that to hate was essentially to murder, since it's the root of murder (v. 21-22). For this reason, when battling sin, we must battle it first on the heart level so that it never manifests as an action.

God has given people the highest standard: We are called to be holy as God is holy (1 Pet 1:16) and perfect as he is perfect (Matt 5:48), which includes not only our actions, but also our words and thoughts. To fail at this, is to sin—to miss the mark of God's glory (Rom 3:23).

Reflection

1. What stood out most in the reading and why?
2. What is a good definition of sin?
3. What are the primary Hebrew and Greek words used for sin and what do they mean?
4. What are a sin of commission and a sin of omission?
5. What questions or applications did you take from the reading?

The Origin of Sin

What is the origin of sin? How did it come into the world? First, it must be said that God did not create sin. In Job 34:10, Elihu, Job's friend, rightly said, "Therefore, listen to me, you men of understanding. Far be it from God to do wickedness, from the Almighty to do evil." Likewise, 1 John 1:5 says, "God is light, and in him there is no darkness at all." God is totally pure; he cannot be corrupted by sin, tempted to sin, and he doesn't tempt anyone to sin (Jam 1:13).

Well then, how was sin introduced into creation? Sin came into being because God created creatures with freedom—the ability to obey or disobey. Why? Scripture never directly says, but the fact that he created creatures with freedom implies that he wanted them to choose rightly. It's like in a marriage. In general, nobody wants someone to be forced to marry them. They want a person to choose of his or her own free volition. God is the same. He commands us to follow and obey him, but he also wants us to choose freely, which is why he commonly informs us of the benefits of obedience and the consequences of disobedience. For example, with Adam and Eve, he told them to not eat of the forbidden tree. If they did, they would know good and evil and eventually die (Gen 2:17). God typically gives us a command, reasons to obey it, including the consequences for disobedience, and the ability to choose whether to obey. God did not want to create robots who had no choice, though he could have. He decided to create creatures that could choose to love, trust, and obey him, which opened the door for sin to happen.

Unfortunately, the creatures that God created chose to rebel against him. The first rebellion happened in heaven. By considering Ezekiel 28:11-19 and other passages, it is clear that Satan was originally a beautiful angel with an exalted position at the throne of God. However, Satan became prideful—wanting to be like God (Is 14:12-14). Therefore, he rebelled, and one-third of the angels rebelled with him. Consequently, Satan and his followers were cast out of heaven (Rev 12:3-4). This was the beginning of sin.

But sin later happened on earth as well. When God created humans, he gave them one prohibition—to not eat of the tree of the knowledge of good and evil (Gen 2:17). The reason he gave them a prohibition was to remind them that they were not God—they were under his rule. Soon after, Satan tempted the first humans with the same temptation he fell to (Gen 3:4-5, Is 14:12-14). He said to Eve that they would be like God if they ate of the tree. Eve, in seeking to be like God (and therefore independent from him), ate of the tree. Then Adam ate of the tree as well, leading the human race into sin and bringing God's creation under a curse.

This is sin's origin. It began in heaven with an angelic rebellion, and it continued on earth when humans rebelled as well.

Why Did God Allow Sin?

Why did God allow sin? Does the advent of sin mean that God ceased to be in control of his creation? Though hard to understand, Scripture teaches that God is omniscient (all-knowing), omnipotent (all-powerful), and sovereign (in control of all things, including evil). This is a mystery that Scripture clearly teaches. Ephesians 1:11 says, God "accomplishes all things according to the counsel of his will." Also, Colossians 1:17 says God is at all times holding all things together by his mighty power—including our solar system, planet, humans, Satan, demons, animals, and plants. This means Satan and the other rebellious angels were never in control. Like all creatures, they are totally dependent upon God for their existence, and yet, by God's sovereign choice, "free" to make decisions.

Though creatures are free to make decisions, God is somehow in control of them. In Job 1 and 2, we see that Satan needed to get permission from God to afflict a man named Job. All the afflictions, including the theft of his goods, death of family members and servants, devastating natural disasters, and physical sickness, though caused by the devil, were all under God's control. Again, Scripture says God "accomplishes all things according to the counsel of his will" (Eph 1:11) and that all things work to the good of those who love the Lord (Rom 8:28). This means the view called dualism, which teaches that in the world there are two competing equal powers—good versus evil—is not true. God is totally in control of Satan and demons. In fact, Scripture teaches that before God created the earth, he chose a remnant of "elect angels" (1 Tim 5:21) who would not rebel against him and an "elect" remnant of people on the earth who would not remain in rebellion—but would repent and follow God. Ephesians 1:4 says, "For he chose us in Christ before the foundation of the world that we may be holy and unblemished in his sight in love." This means that God knew about these future rebellions (with angels and men), planned for them, and allowed them for some greater reason.

Why did God allow these rebellions and the resulting sin and destruction? Scripture gives us a few reasons: (1) Somehow, God allowing sin brings greater glory to himself. Consider a few support texts. Romans 9:22-23 says:

> But what if God, willing to demonstrate his wrath and to make known his power, has endured with much patience the objects of wrath prepared for destruction? And what if he is willing to make known the wealth of his glory on the

objects of mercy that he has prepared beforehand for glory

In describing God's sovereignty over people (both good and bad), Paul said that God is demonstrating his "wrath" and "power" by being patient with the "objects of wrath" (v. 22)—beings who rebel and do evil. Also, with the "objects of mercy" (v. 23)—people who sinned but God saved—God is making his "glory" known through their salvation. Both objects of wrath and objects of mercy allow God to demonstrate different facets of his glory—his wrath, power, and mercy.

In addition, Ephesians 2:7 gives this as one of the reasons God saves sinners who repent: "to demonstrate in the coming ages the surpassing wealth of his grace in kindness toward us in Christ Jesus." God's saving of people who rebel against him will demonstrate his grace—unmerited favor—throughout eternity. It has been said that when the angels rebelled, God demonstrated his holiness and wrath. No mercy was offered to any fallen angel. However, with humanity, God demonstrates his grace—something the angels never saw. God gave unmerited favor to a remnant of people—saving them from their sin and the consequences of it. This demonstrates that God allowed sin to manifest aspects of his glory including his wrath, patience, power, and grace. Like a diamond sparkling more magnificently against a black cloth, God allowed sin to demonstrate his glory and to ultimately bring about great good.

Finally, Ephesians 3:10-11 says this about God's saving of the church—which consists of Jew and Gentile together:

The purpose of this enlightenment is that through the church the multifaceted wisdom of God should now be disclosed to the rulers and the authorities in the heavenly realms. This was according to the eternal purpose that he accomplished in Christ Jesus our Lord,

God's work in saving the church (sinners who repent and believe in God) will not only demonstrate his grace—unmerited favor—but also his "multifaceted wisdom" throughout eternity (v. 10). To take the mess that rebellious angels and humans created and make it glorious will show God's tremendous wisdom.

In eternity, before creation, God could see millions of different options and ways things could have turned out, and yet, he chose to allow the current one. On this side of eternity, especially when considering how corrupt things are and have been, it may not make sense, but one day, we will all fall down and declare that God is glorious, merciful, gracious, and wise. He knows what is best, and we can trust that he chose the best plan which would bring glory to himself and bless his people (Rom 8:28).

Certainly, we see a perfect display of this in the gospel. Jesus, the Son of God, was murdered by evil people, which is the greatest crime ever committed. However, God took the worst thing that ever happened and made it the greatest thing that ever happened, as God saves people through the death and resurrection of his Son. Even this evil event was planned before time and allowed by God for the greatest good. In Acts 2:23, Peter said this to those who murdered Christ, "this man, who was handed over by the predetermined plan and foreknowledge of God, you executed by nailing him to a cross at the hands of Gentiles." Surely when it is all said and done, God will be proven to be truly wise, omnipotent, and glorious, as he allows and uses sin for a greater purpose.

Reflection

1. What stood out most in the reading and why?
2. Where did sin come from?
3. Why did God allow sin?

4. What other questions or applications did you take from the reading?

The Effects of Sin

How did Adam's sin affect humanity? His disobedience affected the human race in at least two ways:

1. Because of Adam's sin, the human race inherits his guilt.

    Romans 5:12, 17, and 19 says,

    So then, just as sin entered the world through one man and death through sin, and so death spread to all people because all sinned... For if, by the transgression of the one man, death reigned through the one, how much more will those who receive the abundance of grace and of the gift of righteousness reign in life through the one, Jesus Christ!... For just as through the disobedience of the one man many were made sinners, so also through the obedience of one man many will be made righteous.

    God promised Adam and Eve that if they ate of the tree, they would die (Gen 2:17). Death really just means "separation." In physical death, the body is separated from the soul. Eventually, in Genesis 5, Adam and Eve died physically. But there are also two other types of death: spiritual death and eternal death. After Adam and Eve sinned and when God was looking for them in the garden, they hid from him (Gen 3:8). They experienced spiritual death—separation from intimacy with God and his goodness. Now, all people hide from God. In Romans 1:21-23, Paul said this about the ancient world,

For although they knew God, they did not glorify him as God or give him thanks, but they became futile in their thoughts and their senseless hearts were darkened. Although they claimed to be wise, they became fools and exchanged the glory of the immortal God for an image resembling mortal human beings or birds or four-footed animals or reptiles.

Like Adam and Eve who hid from God, people know there is a God because of an innate, God-given conscience that all people have (Rom 1:19, 2:15) and also because of creation's witness. Paul said because of creation people are without excuse for believing in God (Rom 1:20, cf. Ps 19:1-6). However, instead of acknowledging God, people hide from him by ignoring God to focus on themselves, creating idols to worship instead of God, or denying his existence altogether. That is the state of people before salvation—spiritual death. And if people continue in spiritual death without repenting and following Christ, they will eventually experience eternal death—separation from God's goodness in hell forever. Since God is omnipresent, he is present everywhere, at all times, including hell. However, in hell, he is present only to judge eternally and never to bless. In hell, there will be no grace, mercy, love, or goodness. Revelation 20:15 describes this final judgment when it says, "If anyone's name was not found written in the book of life, that person was thrown into the lake of fire." Because of Adam's sin, the human race, now, experiences spiritual, physical, and eternal death. The only hope for us is Jesus, God's Son, who experienced death for us so that we could experience eternal life.

Now what must be noticed in Romans 5 is that even though all people sin and earn death on their own (Roman 3:23, 6:23), we are first of all guilty because of Adam's sin. Romans 5:12 says because of one man's sin, "death spread to all people because all sinned." All people "sinned"—past tense—in and through Adam, including those who have not been born yet, and therefore experience his guilt, including death. Likewise, Romans 5:17 says "For if, by the transgression of the one man, death reigned through the one." All die because of one man named Adam. Further proof that all people experience Adam's guilt is the fact that even infants die, though never sinning willfully.

How is it possible that all "sinned" in Adam? There are two primary views:

- One view is called *federal head theory*. In federal head theory, Adam represented all of humanity before God, even as kings, presidents, and prime ministers represent certain people groups today. As the federal head, when Adam sinned against God, he essentially declared war with God. And because he declared war with God, all his offspring are included in that war. Though this may not seem fair, it's the same with wars today. When the king, president, or prime minister declares war, the people in that nation are at war, even those who disagree with it. God made Adam our king, and we sinned and rebelled against God when he did. Doctrinally, this act is called imputation. Adam's sin is credited to our account because of him being our leader; therefore, we all are guilty and experience the resulting consequence, which is death.

- Another view is called *realistic theory* or *natural theory*. It is also sometimes called the Augustinian view. Augustine believed humanity sinned when Adam sinned because humanity was in Adam's loins when it happened. Biblical support for this view is seen in Hebrews when the writer describes Melchizedek's priesthood as greater than the Levitical priesthood (7:1-10). The author argues based on the fact that Levi was Abraham's grandson, and Abraham paid tithes to the ancient priest Melchizedek (Gen 14). Levi, though unborn, essentially paid tithes to

Melchizedek through Abraham, as "he was still in his ancestor Abraham's loins" (Heb 7:9-10). Therefore, since the lesser typically pays tithes to the greater, the priesthood of Melchizedek is greater than that of Levi. Thus, Augustine believed all of humanity likewise "sinned" in the loins of Adam, and consequently received his same punishment. Though there is merit to the Augustinian view, the federal headship has been more widely accepted throughout history.

Now again, many would vigorously declare, "This is not fair! How can we be punished because of the sin of Adam?" (1) It should be remembered that though we all die because of Adam's sin, we all sin like Adam and therefore deserve death. Again, unless we die as infants, we all rebel against God in our thoughts, words, and actions. Romans 3:23 says, "for all have sinned and fall short of the glory of God," and Romans 6:23 says, "the payoff of sin is death." Apart from Adam's transferred guilt, we earn death because of our own sins. (2) Another thing we must consider when trying to understand Adam's sin being imputed to us is Scripture's teaching that when we repent and follow Christ, his righteous life is imputed to ours, which is why God saves us from the penalty of our sins. Romans 5:19 says, "For just as through the disobedience of the one man many were made sinners, so also through the obedience of one man many will be made righteous." In this way, Christ is called the "last Adam" (1 Cor 15:45). The first federal head led us into sin and death, but the second one leads us into righteousness and eternal life. If we think it is unfair for Adam's sins to be imputed to us, we must also consider it unfair for Christ's righteousness to be imputed to us (2 Cor 5:21). God regards the human race as an organic unity under Adam, and Christians—those who repent and believe in Christ—as an organic unity under Christ.[4]

How else did Adam's sin affect humanity?

2. Because of Adam's sin, the human race inherits his sinful disposition.

This is often called "original sin" or "inherited sin."[5] It is original because it traces back to Adam's original sin. After Adam's sin, he then had a sinful disposition—a sin nature—and all his children inherit it as well. R. C. Sproul describes original sin this way:

> Original sin describes our fallen, sinful condition, out of which actual sins occur. Scripture does not tell us that we are sinners because we sin; rather, it affirms that we sin because we are sinners. We have a fallen, corrupt nature, out of which flow the actual sins we commit. Original sin, then, describes the fallen condition of the human race.[6]

Though people tend to think of humanity's sinfulness as a product of environment—something learned—that simply is not true. Scripture says we are born with this sinful tendency. In Psalm 51:5, David said: "Look, I was guilty of sin from birth, a sinner the moment my mother conceived me." From conception, in the womb, children are sinful. They are born as little tyrants—wanting their own way. As they become toddlers, they cry, scream, yell, fall on the floor, and hit if they don't get their way. They don't have to be taught to do wrong. They discover that on their own. They have to be taught to do good. Likewise, Psalm 58:3 says, "The wicked turn aside from birth; liars go astray as soon as they are born."

Total Depravity

The effects of sin on human nature are widespread and total in scope. Sin has affected every aspect of humanity, including the mind, will, and emotions. This is called the doctrine of total depravity. "Depravity" simply means "corruption." In Romans 7:18, Paul said: "For I know that nothing good lives in me, that is, in my flesh. For I want to do the good, but I cannot do it." Often in Scripture, our sinful nature is called the "flesh" or the "old man" (Rom 8:5, 6:6). In the flesh, there is a continual inclination to sin against God and others. Galatians 5:19-21 describes this:

> Now the works of the flesh are obvious: sexual immorality, impurity, depravity, idolatry, sorcery, hostilities, strife, jealousy, outbursts of anger, selfish rivalries, dissensions, factions, envying, murder, drunkenness, carousing, and similar things. I am warning you, as I had warned you before: Those who practice such things will not inherit the kingdom of God!

Likewise, Jeremiah 17:9 (NIV) says, "The heart is deceitful above all things and beyond cure. Who can understand it?" In fact, sin has affected the human mind and emotions in such a way that people, apart from God's grace, cannot understand God's Word or submit to it. Romans 8:7 says, "the outlook of the flesh is hostile to God, for it does not submit to the law of God, nor is it able to do so." Also, 1 Corinthians 2:14 says, "The unbeliever does not receive the things of the Spirit of God, for they are foolishness to him. And he cannot understand them, because they are spiritually discerned."

Because the effects of sin are so debilitating on the human will, God must do a supernatural work in a person's life for him or her to be saved at all. In John 6:44, Christ said, "No one can come to me unless the Father who sent me draws him, and I will raise him up at the last day." And, Ephesians 2:8-9 says, "For by grace you are saved through faith, and this is not from yourselves, it is the gift of God; it is not from works, so that no one can boast." Since the flesh—our natural disposition—is hostile to God and cannot obey him (Rom 8:7) and the fact that our unredeemed minds cannot understand or accept God's Word (1 Cor 2:14), God must act to save us. Salvation is by grace—unmerited favor—and includes God giving people faith to be saved (Eph 2:8-9, Phil 1:29). Paul rightly described unbelievers as "dead" in their "transgressions and sins" (Eph 2:1). As dead people, they cannot respond to spiritual stimuli. God must act by drawing them to himself and giving them faith to positively respond to the gospel message (John 6:44).

Total depravity essentially means three things:

1. Because of humanity's sin nature, the mind, will, and emotions of every person have been corrupted. Again, in Romans 7:18, Paul said, "For I know that nothing good lives in me, that is, in my flesh." This taints everything one does—thoughts, words, and deeds.

2. Because of humanity's sin nature, people can do nothing that pleases God, apart from grace. This is taught in various texts: Isaiah 64:6 says, "We are all like one who is unclean, all our so-called righteous acts are like a menstrual rag in your sight." Even our good deeds are tainted by sin before God. This is because, though humans do many good deeds, their heart motives in doing them are corrupt. For example, Hebrews 11:6 says, "without faith it is impossible to please" God. Since unbelievers are not trusting in God nor seeking to bring him glory by what they do, they can't please God. Also, in John 15:5, Christ said that by abiding in him, we'll produce much fruit, but apart from him, we can do nothing. Again, this means people, apart from Christ, can do nothing pleasing to God. It's our being attached to Christ which makes our works acceptable. Therefore, total depravity means that people, apart from saving and sanctifying grace, can do nothing that pleases God or earns merit with him.

3. Because of humanity's sin nature, people can do nothing to save themselves. Though humans are free to make choices, their choices are driven by their nature. Again, in Romans 8:7, Paul said, "the outlook of the flesh is hostile to God, for it does not submit to the law of God, nor is it able to do so." Apart from God graciously drawing us to himself and equipping us to respond, nobody will choose God. Like animals, humans always act according to their nature. If you offer a lion steak or salad, 100 out of 100 times he will choose steak because of his nature. Likewise, our sinful nature causes us to reject Christ and choose sin. Therefore, to be saved, God must graciously act by choosing us, providing an opportunity to hear the gospel, and giving us faith to respond to it (cf. Rom 8:29-30, Eph 1:4, 2:8-9, Phil 1:29). Ephesians 2:8-9 says, "For by grace you are saved through faith, and this is not from yourselves, it is the gift of God; it is not from works, so that no one can boast." Because of the total depravity of our nature, people cannot contribute to their salvation, unlike what most religions teach, including Roman Catholicism. Salvation must be completely by grace—unmerited favor from God.

With that said, total depravity does not mean everybody is as bad as they could be. Wayne Grudem's comments on this are helpful:

This inherited tendency to sin does not mean that human beings are all as bad as they could be. The constraints of civil law, the expectations of family and society, and the conviction of human conscience (Rom. 2:14–15) all provide restraining influences on the sinful tendencies in our hearts. Therefore, by God's "common grace" (that is, by his undeserved favor that is given to all human beings), people have been able to do much good in the areas of education, the development of civilization, scientific and technological progress, the development of beauty and skill in the arts, the development of just laws, and general acts of human benevolence and kindness to others.[2]

All people, including unsaved ones, (1) are made in the image of God (Gen 1:27), (2) have a God-given conscience, though imperfect, which convicts them of sin and affirms their good deeds (Rom 2:15), and (3) are recipients of God's common grace, as God provides many good things for them—life, breath, sunshine, rain, etc.—so that they will seek him (Acts 17:5, Matt 5:45). Therefore, people have a tremendous capacity to do good, and have done so; however, apart from God's saving grace which gives them a new nature, they cannot please God or have ultimate victory over sin.

Reflection

1. What stood out most in the reading and why?
2. What were the effects of Adam's sin on the human race?
3. What are the federal head theory of sin and the realistic/natural theory?
4. What does the term original sin mean?
5. What is total depravity and what are its implications for the human condition?
6. What other questions or applications did you take from the reading?

Degrees of Sin

Are some sins worse than other sins? Yes, and no. There are two things that we must consider when answering this question:

1. As for our legal standing, all sin separates us from God and makes us eternally guilty.

    Romans 3:23 says, "the payoff of sin is death." Again, death simply means separation. This was true with Adam and Eve. Because of their sin, they died. They were separated from God both spiritually and physically, and this is still true today. Sin separates us from God whether that be a "small sin" or a "large sin." James 2:10-11 says:

    > For the one who obeys the whole law but fails in one point has become guilty of all of it. For he who said, "Do not commit adultery," also said, "Do not murder." Now if you do not commit adultery but do commit murder, you have become a violator of the law.

    If we break one of God's laws, we break the whole law. James pictures God's law as a mirror or chain; if part of it is broken, all of it is broken. In a legal sense, every sin breaks the entirety of God's law, and since all people are sinners, we equally stand before God as lawbreakers.

2. As for our life and relationships with God and others, some sins are worse in the sense of them having greater consequences.

In the sense of consequences, coveting a neighbor's car is not as bad as stealing it. And likewise, slandering someone is not as bad as murdering him. In that sense, some sins are greater than others. Also, though all sin displeases God, certain sins will arouse his displeasure more, interrupt our fellowship with him more, and merit greater consequences from him. For example, God is more displeased with those who sin with full knowledge of how bad something is and its consequences than those who sin without that awareness. In Luke 12:47-48, Christ said this:

> That servant who knew his master's will but did not get ready or do what his master asked will receive a severe beating. But the one who did not know his master's will and did things worthy of punishment will receive a light beating. From everyone who has been given much, much will be required, and from the one who has been entrusted with much, even more will be asked.

This also probably demonstrates why James says that those who teach will receive a stricter judgment from God (Jam 3:1). Their knowledge of what is right and teaching it makes them more responsible before God than an immature believer.

In addition, Scripture teaches that some of God's commands, though equally God's Word, are weightier than others. In Matthew 5:19, Christ said: "So anyone who breaks one of the least of these commands and teaches others to do so will be called least in the kingdom of heaven." In addition, Christ rebuked the Pharisees for their keen focus on things like tithing but neglecting the "more important in the law—justice, mercy, and faithfulness!" (Matt 23:23). The Pharisees were right for giving their tithes but not to the exclusion of justice, mercy, and faithfulness. If a person is giving tithes but cheating others and condemning the righteous, what good is the tithe? The fact that Christ taught that some teachings were greater than others implies that some sins are worse than others. Again, certainly murdering someone is worse than gossiping about them.

Wayne Grudem gives several reasons why it may be important to distinguish between degrees of sin:

1. "First, it helps us to know where we should put more effort in our own attempts to grow in personal holiness.

2. Second, it helps us to decide when we should simply overlook a minor fault in a friend or family member and when it would be appropriate to talk with an individual about some evident sin (see James 5:19–20).

3. Third, it may help us decide when church discipline is appropriate, and it provides an answer to the objection that is sometimes raised against exercising church discipline, in which it is said that 'we are all guilty of sin, so we have no business meddling in anyone else's life.' Though we are all indeed guilty of sin, nonetheless, there are some sins that so evidently harm the church and relationships within the church that they must be dealt with directly.

4. Fourth, this distinction may also help us realize that there is some basis for civil governments to have laws and penalties prohibiting certain kinds of wrongdoing (such as murder or stealing), but not other kinds of wrongdoing (such as anger, jealousy, greed, or selfish use of one's possessions). It is not inconsistent to say that some kinds of wrongdoing require civil punishment but not all kinds of wrongdoing require it."[7] (numbering added for emphasis)

Reflection

1. What stood out most to you in the reading and why?
2. Are all sins equal in God's sight? Why or why not?
3. Why is it important to distinguish between degrees of sin?
4. Are some doctrines more important than others (cf. Matt 5:19, 23:23)? If so, how can we discern which are major or minor doctrines (or even primary, secondary, or tertiary doctrines)? Also, what are the implications for fellowshipping or breaking fellowship with other believers over such things (cf. Gal 1:8)?
5. What other questions or applications did you take from the reading?

The Unpardonable Sin and The Sin Resulting in Death

What are the unpardonable sin (or the blasphemy of the Spirit) and the sin resulting in death? We'll consider the unpardonable sin first. In the context of the Pharisees declaring that Christ was doing miracles through the devil's power, Christ said:

> For this reason I tell you, people will be forgiven for every sin and blasphemy, but the blasphemy against the Spirit will not be forgiven. Whoever speaks a word against the Son of Man will be forgiven. But whoever speaks against the Holy Spirit will not be forgiven, either in this age or in the age to come.
> Matthew 12:31-32

What is the blasphemy of the Spirit, which can never be forgiven? There are numerous views on what this actually means:

1. Some believe the blasphemy of the Spirit is something that can never happen today. They focus on the context of the Pharisees declaring that Christ's miracles were done through Satan instead of the Holy Spirit. Since Christ is no longer physically on the earth doing miracles, that sin cannot happen anymore.

2. Some believe the blasphemy of the Spirit is unbelief. Those who persist in unbelief and therefore reject Christ

as their Lord and Savior will never be forgiven. Certainly, this is true, but it doesn't seem to clearly reflect the context in which Christ said this.

3. Some believe the blasphemy of the Spirit is a sin only certain unbelievers can commit. It is the sin of those who have experienced tremendous, repeated exposure to the witness of God's Word and his Spirit but continually reject it. They typically profess faith in God and associate with a body of believers but are not truly saved. Their repeated exposure to the truth and rejection of it eventually hardens their hearts to the point where they cannot repent, and consequently, they will never be forgiven by God.

It seems that the third view is to be preferred, when considering the context and other similar Scriptures. The Pharisees not only heard God's Word through Christ, but also studied and taught the Mosaic law, as Israel's spiritual leaders. Also, as Christ mentioned, their "sons" (other Jews under their leadership) even cast out demons (Matt 12:27)—presumably by the same Holy Spirit that Christ cast them out. However, though the Pharisees had great exposure to God's Word and God's Spirit, they still rejected God and therefore hardened their hearts to the point of no return.

This seems to correspond to how Christ responded to the Israelites, whom the Pharisees represented, in the next chapter of Matthew. In Matthew 13, after the leaders of Israel rejected Christ's ministry, Christ changed his method of teaching. Instead of clearly teaching God's Word, he started to teach in parables, which hid the truth from the hearers. After this change, the disciples asked him why he was teaching in parables. Christ said this in response:

He replied, "You have been given the opportunity to know the secrets of the kingdom of heaven, but they have not. For whoever has will be given more, and will have an abundance. But whoever does not have, even what he has will be taken from him. For this reason I speak to them in parables: Although they see they do not see, and although they hear they do not hear nor do they understand. And concerning them the prophecy of Isaiah is fulfilled that says: 'You will listen carefully yet will never understand, you will look closely yet will never comprehend. For the heart of this people has become dull; they are hard of hearing, and they have shut their eyes, so that they would not see with their eyes and hear with their ears and understand with their hearts and turn, and I would heal them.'
Matthew 13:11-15

If this corresponds with the blasphemy of the Spirit, which it seems to because of the context, the Pharisees' sin had to do with receiving God's revelation and continually rejecting it. Christ says, "For whoever has will be given more, and will have abundance. But whoever does not have, even what he has will be taken from him" (13:12). Then, Christ quotes Isaiah and how Israel would become dull of heart, hard of hearing, and blind, so they would not repent and be saved (v. 14-15). They would not be forgiven because they would not repent. Israel and their leaders had seen Christ's miracles, heard his Word, and some had even taught God's Word and possibly done miracles, yet they still rejected the Spirit's work. Consequently, they had hardened their hearts and blasphemed the Holy Spirit; therefore, they would never repent and never be forgiven.

Many also connect the blasphemy of the Holy Spirit with the difficult passage of Hebrews 6:4-6. It says,

For it is impossible in the case of those who have once been enlightened, tasted the heavenly gift, become partakers of the Holy Spirit, tasted the good word of God and the miracles of the coming age, and then have committed apostasy, to renew them again to repentance, since they are crucifying the Son of God for themselves all over again and holding him up to contempt.

The Hebrew Christians, in this context, were being tempted to reject all they had learned and experienced in Christianity to return to Judaism. The writer warns them if they reject Christ after tasting God's Word, experiencing the Holy Spirit and his miracles, it will become impossible for them to repent (v. 6). Though some believe this text refers to believers actually losing their salvation, the whole counsel of Scripture seems to indicate that is not possible. For true believers, God gives them "eternal life" (John 3:16). Christ puts them in his hand and God's hand, and nobody will be able to snatch them out (John 10:27-29). Christ came to do the Father's will and his will is that those given to Christ by God would not be lost but raised up on the last day (John 6:38-39). To do this, Christ not only holds believers in his hand, but he also prays daily for them so he can save them to the uttermost (Heb 7:25). Therefore, if a professed follower turns away from God, it proves they were never truly saved. Like Christ said, though they may call him, "Lord, Lord," he will say to them, "I never knew you. Go away from me, you lawbreakers!" (Matt 7:23).

If the professing Christians in Hebrews 6 did in fact turn away from God after all they had experienced (God's Word, his Spirit, the powers of the coming age, etc.), they would be just like the Pharisees and the Jews in Matthew 12 and 13. They identified with God's people, professed him, served him, learned his Word, taught his Word, and possibly even did miracles like casting out demons, but because they never truly repented, their continued rejection of God hardened their hearts, making it impossible for them to repent. They had blasphemed the Spirit.

Because of this, it should be understood that if a person thinks that he somehow committed the unforgivable sin of blaspheming the Holy Spirit, but still desires to repent and follow God, it means that he has not committed this sin. A person who committed this sin will not want to repent, which is why he will never be forgiven (Heb 6:6).

Another potential example of blaspheming the Spirit is the apostle Judas. Christ gave him power to heal and cast out demons (Lk 9:1). He preached the gospel in various villages (Lk 9:6), and yet throughout his time following Christ, he continually stole from the disciples (John 12:6) and eventually betrayed Christ (Lk 22:47-48). Though Scripture never says he committed the unforgivable sin, the characteristics mentioned in Hebrews 6:4-6 are true of him. He had been enlightened, partook of the Holy Spirit, tasted of the heavenly gift, the word of God, and the miracles of the coming age, and yet committed apostasy. Though he professed Christ and served him, Scripture teaches that he never was a true born-again believer and actually calls him a "devil" (John 6:70). No doubt, his continual exposure to and rejection of the things of God only further hardened his heart—hindering his ability to ultimately repent (Matt 13:12, 15, Heb 6:6).

The Sin Resulting in Death

Several passages also describe something called a "sin resulting in death." For example, John 5:16-17 says,

If anyone sees his fellow Christian committing a sin not resulting in death, he should ask, and God will grant life to the person who commits a sin not resulting in death. There is a sin resulting in death. I do not say that he should ask about that. All unrighteousness is sin, but there is sin not resulting in death.

Also, James 5:19-20 may be referring to this, when it says,

> My brothers and sisters, if anyone among you wanders from the truth and someone turns him back, he should know that the one who turns a sinner back from his wandering path will save that person's soul from death and will cover a multitude of sins.

The sin resulting in death refers to God allowing unrepentant believers to die early as a form of discipline. An example of this is seen in the story of Ananias and Saphira. In Acts 5:1-10, this married couple sold their land and gave the proceeds to the apostles as a gift. However, they lied and said they gave all the proceeds when they had really kept back a portion of it (even though they were under no pressure to give any of it). Because of this public sin, probably inspired by pride and their desire to be revered by all, God struck them dead. Also, in 1 Corinthians 11, the believers were taking the Lord's Supper in a dishonorable manner, with drunkenness and division (v. 20-22). Because of that, God judged some by taking them home. First Corinthians 11:30-32 says, "That is why many of you are weak and sick, and quite a few are dead. But if we examined ourselves, we would not be judged. But when we are judged by the Lord, we are disciplined so that we may not be condemned with the world."

The sin resulting in death is a form of God's discipline, in which he corrects believers and helps them become holy. Hebrews 12:5-6 (NIV) says,

> And have you completely forgotten this word of encouragement that addresses you as a father addresses his son? It says, "My son, do not make light of the Lord's discipline, and do not lose heart when he rebukes you, because the Lord disciplines the one he loves, and he chastens everyone he accepts as his son."

In these verses, "discipline" seems to be a general word for how God corrects his children, and "rebukes" and "chastens" seem to be two of the methods. When we are in sin, God rebukes us through his Word, often given through other saints—seeking to turn us away from sin. Then, if we don't respond, eventually he chastens us, which literally means "whips" or "spanks." Because of continued rebellion against his rebukes, God brings whippings, often appearing in trials to turn us away from wrong attitudes and actions. At times though, if we continue to persist in sin or commit a specific sin which is particularly grievous, the "whipping" may be as severe as taking one of his saints home. This is the sin resulting in death.

Reflection

1. What stood out most in the reading and why?
2. What are the various views about the unpardonable sin? Which view do you think is correct and why?
3. What is the sin resulting in death? How should the reality of this sin and its discipline affect us and how we relate to others in sin?
4. What other questions or applications did you take from the reading?

The Remedy for Sin

What is the remedy for our sin nature? We've considered how we are totally depraved—meaning that every aspect of our human nature has been corrupted by sin to such a degree that we can do nothing pleasing to God because of our rebellious nature, and we cannot save ourselves. Therefore, God must save us. However, in our salvation, God gave believers several remedies to conquer their sin nature.

1. On the cross, the sin nature of believers was crucified with Christ, and though it remains with us, we've been delivered from slavery to it.

Romans 6:6 says, "We know that our old man was crucified with him so that the body of sin would no longer dominate us, so that we would no longer be enslaved to sin." On the cross, Christ not only paid the penalty for our sin, but delivered us from slavery to it, so that we could be slaves of God and righteousness instead (6:18).

Because of this reality, in Romans 6:11, Paul says, "So you too consider yourselves dead to sin, but alive to God in Christ Jesus." We must think of ourselves differently. Possibly before being saved, we thought that it was impossible to be delivered from a certain tendency or practice that had identified us for years or possibly our entire lives. That tendency might be anger, unforgiveness, anxiety, or a sexual orientation. A common lie planted by Satan through the world and our flesh is that this tendency is just who we are and that it cannot or should not change. Accepting this type of lie actually hinders the Holy Spirit's ability to make us more like Christ (cf. Acts 7:51). As Paul said, we must recognize what Christ did for us on the cross, so we can become slaves of righteousness instead of slaves of sin (Rom 6:18).

2. At salvation, God gives believers a new nature, empowered by the Holy Spirit, to conquer sin.

Nature refers to a tendency or capacity within a person towards something.[8] Unbelievers only have a sin nature, which is a tendency towards evil. It's not that unbelievers can't do good—it's just that their good works are tainted by sinful motives. However, at salvation, believers become new creations in Christ and receive a new nature, empowered by God's Spirit (Col 3:10, 2 Cor 5:17). They gain a desire and ability to do what is righteous (cf. Matt 5:6, Phil 2:12-13). Because of this, in believers there is a continual battle between their two opposing natures. In Galatians 5:16-17, Paul describes this, when he says,

> But I say, live by the Spirit and you will not carry out the desires of the flesh. For the flesh has desires that are opposed to the Spirit, and the Spirit has desires that are opposed to the flesh, for these are in opposition to each other, so that you cannot do what you want.

This battle often results in believers sinning—doing what they don't want to do. In Romans 7:19-20, Paul describes this: "For I do not do the good I want, but I do the very evil I do not want! Now if I do what I do not want, it is no longer me doing it but sin that lives in me." However, in Galatians 5:16, Paul offers battle-weary believers a remedy. He says, if we "live by the Spirit," we will "not carry out the desires of the flesh." It can also be translated "walk by the Spirit." This pictures step by step, moment by moment, dependence upon the Lord for victory over our sinful desires.

How can we walk by the Spirit? We do this by continually obeying God's will for our life, especially as we practice spiritual disciplines such as prayer, thanksgiving, reading God's Word, engaging in Christian community and worship, serving others, and turning from sin. As we do this moment by moment, hour by hour, and day by day, we experience victories over our sinful nature.

Often this battle between our new nature and sin nature has been described as battles between two starving dogs. Which starving dog will win? The dog that we feed. If we feed our flesh ungodly entertainment, conversations, and evil attitudes and acts, the flesh will win. But if we feed our new nature (and starve our flesh), our new nature will win.

3. When we sin, we should confess our sins to the Lord and accept his forgiveness.

In the Lord's Prayer, Christ taught believers to ask God for forgiveness (Matt 6:12). And in 1 John 1:9, John says, "But if we confess our sins, he is faithful and righteous, forgiving us our sins and cleansing us from all unrighteousness." To "confess" means "to say the same thing."[9] It is in the present tense, which means it is not referring to a "once-for-all confession of sin at our conversion" (cf. Acts 20:21).[10] It means that believers should continually confess every wrong thought, word, and action to God. To confess does not just mean to recognize something as sin before God, but also to despise and turn away from it. In response, God forgives us and cleanses us from all unrighteousness.

If God forgave all our sins on the cross, why do we still need to confess them when we sin? On the cross, God forgave our sins judicially. We will never pay for our sins eternally because they were paid for on the cross by Christ. However, when we sin after salvation, we need to seek relational forgiveness. For example, when I sin against my wife, it doesn't change our legal status—she remains my wife. However, my sin does negatively affect our fellowship. When I confess, it restores our fellowship. Likewise, when we sin, we turn away from God and can't enjoy his blessing and intimacy as we previously did. When we turn back, our relationship is rightly aligned and restored. Therefore, we should continually confess our sins, which include turning from them back to God.

4. At death, God will remove our sin nature.

When we die and our bodies are separated from our spirit, our sin nature will be gone as well; therefore, we will no longer struggle with sin. In Hebrews 12:23, believers who have died and are waiting in heaven for their resurrection are called the "spirits of the righteous, who have been made perfect." Then one day, God will give us glorified bodies at Christ's return. In Philippians 3:20-21, Paul said this:

> But our citizenship is in heaven—and we also await a savior from there, the Lord Jesus Christ, who will transform these humble bodies of ours into the likeness of his glorious body by means of that power by which he is able to subject all things to himself.

God has done many things in the believers' salvation to deliver them from their sin nature: He broke the power of sin on the cross, so we no longer would be slaves to it. He gave us a new nature, empowered by God's Spirit. He forgives our sins when we confess them—restoring our intimacy with God. Finally, at our death or the rapture (whichever happens first), God will deliver us from the presence of our sin nature.

Perfectionism

Some think that believers can reach perfection—where they will never sin anymore—on this earth. They argue that God would never give commands that believers are unable to keep. If so, that would be unfair. How can God command us to, "Be holy as I am holy," or as Christ commands, "Be perfect as God is perfect," if it were not possible? Therefore, they would say, "If God commands us to do something, he empowers us to do so! So, perfection is surely possible!" Some might even teach that on this earth we can eradicate our sin nature altogether. This belief has at times been taught in Wesleyan traditions. Often, they would say that after some second work of the Spirit (sometimes called the baptism of the Spirit), believers can achieve holiness or perfection.

However, this contradicts what Scripture clearly teaches. It is very possible for God to give us a standard that cannot be achieved. For example, God gave the Israelites the law of Moses, not because they could keep it, but because they couldn't. In fact, God gave provisions (sacrifices) within the law because they would fail at keeping it. Paul taught that the law was a tutor to prepare people for Christ—their need for a savior (Gal 3:24). Therefore, in the New Covenant, God can still command something of us that we cannot attain in our earthly bodies. We are to seek to be like God for the rest of our lives, though we won't achieve it until we get to heaven or Christ returns (Heb 12:23, 1 John 3:2).

Further support that we cannot achieve perfection on earth is seen in the Lord's Prayer, which Christ gave to his saints as a pattern for daily prayer. We are to pray, "forgive us our debts, as we ourselves have forgiven our debtors" (Matt 6:12). The fact that this was included in our pattern of prayer, implies that we will continually need to pray this, just as each of the other petitions: your name be hallowed, your kingdom come, give us our daily bread, and lead us not into temptation but deliver us from the evil one.

In addition, to claim perfection is to claim something that no apostle or godly person in Scripture ever claimed. In Romans 7:15-20, Paul essentially says, "The things that I want to do, I don't do, and the things I don't want to do, I do. Who can save me from this body of sin?" (paraphrase). In Philippians 3:12, Paul said, "Not that I have already attained this—that is, I have not already been perfected—but I strive to lay hold of that for which Christ Jesus also laid hold of me." In James 3:2, James declared, "For we all stumble in many ways." Ecclesiastes 7:20 says, "For there is not one truly righteous person on the earth who continually does good and never sins."

Furthermore, John said, "If we claim to be without sin, we deceive ourselves and the truth is not in us" (1 John 1:8). Throughout the book, John gave tests of true salvation (1 John 5:13), and to him claiming perfection proved that "the truth" (God's Word) was not in a professing believer—that he or she was not truly saved. Truly knowing God actually makes us more aware and sensitive to our sin (cf. Is 6:1-5, Rom 7:15-20). If we claim perfection, then we don't truly know God (1 John 1:8, 1 John 5:13).

It is clear from Scripture that no one will achieve perfection on this earth. We will not be perfect until we get to heaven or Christ returns (Heb 12:23, 1 John 3:2).

Reflection

1. What stood out most in the reading and why?
2. What remedies has God given to conquer our sin nature?
3. What is the view called perfectionism? Why is it not true?
4. What other questions or applications did you take from the reading?

What Happens to Infants When They Die?

What happens to infants when they die is a question that Scripture doesn't clearly answer. What can be clearly said is that (1) infants bear Adam's guilt just like everybody else, which is why they die, even as we do (Rom 5:12, 18-19). (2) They are also born with a sin nature (cf. Ps 51:5, 58:3, Jer 17:9). However, what makes the infant question difficult is that they have never willfully sinned as all other humans have (Rom 3:23, 6:23).

Though Scripture never clearly addresses what happens to infants when they die, there are evidences that seem to indicate that God graciously saves them. The clearest evidence is probably David's response to the death of his infant. While his child was alive and dying, David sought the Lord for mercy by fasting, praying, and mourning. But, when his child died, he stopped. His servants asked, "Why?" David responded:

> While the child was still alive, I fasted and wept because I thought, 'Perhaps the LORD will show pity and the child will live. But now he is dead. Why should I fast? Am I able to bring him back? I will go to him, but he cannot return to me!'
> 2 Samuel 12:22-23

When David says, "I will go to him," he doesn't seem to be simply talking about his future death, but of the reality that he would see his son again. David had a strong belief in heaven. In

Psalm 17:15, he declared that after his death he would behold God's face. And in Psalm 23:6, after declaring that God was his shepherd, David also declared how he would dwell in the house of the Lord forever. It seems that David believed he would see his son again in heaven.

In addition, another potential evidence for God graciously saving infants is the fact that Scripture indicates that people will be eternally judged based on their sins, which infants have never consciously committed. For example, in 1 Corinthians 6:9-10, Paul describes how people are judged for their sins when he says,

> Do you not know that the unrighteous will not inherit the kingdom of God? Do not be deceived! The sexually immoral, idolaters, adulterers, passive homosexual partners, practicing homosexuals, thieves, the greedy, drunkards, the verbally abusive, and swindlers will not inherit the kingdom of God.

Likewise, Revelation 20:12 says,

> And I saw the dead, the great and the small, standing before the throne. Then books were opened, and another book was opened—the book of life. So the dead were judged by what was written in the books, according to their deeds.

Also, people are judged for their rejection of God in general. In Romans 1:20, Paul said because of the witness of creation all people are "without excuse" for believing in God. However, infants, and those with severe developmental needs, do have an excuse. Can those who have never sinned consciously by rejecting God and breaking his commands be justly condemned?

Furthermore, some have seen evidence for God graciously saving infants in Christ's words to the disciples about young children. In Matthew 19:14, Christ said, "Let the little children come to me and do not try to stop them, for the kingdom of heaven belongs to such as these." This word for "children" was used of young children, from infant to toddler age[11] —an age at which they could not exercise saving faith because of mental ability. In the Luke 18:15 parallel passage, it says, "people were even bringing their babies" to Christ. When Christ says, "the kingdom of heaven belongs to such as these," some commentators see this as only referring to how people with childlike faith enter the kingdom. Others believe it also refers to how the kingdom is filled with many young children. John MacArthur said this about the kingdom of heaven belonging "to such as these":

> The implication of such as these is that for those who, because of young age or mental deficiency, are incapable of exercising saving faith, God grants them, in the event of death, entrance into the kingdom by the sovereign operation of His grace. When children die before they reach the age of decision, they go into the presence of Jesus Christ, because they are under the special protection of the sovereign King.[12]

Finally, a logical evidence for God saving infants is simply understanding God's character. Not only is God holy and just, but also good, loving, and merciful, with a special care for the weak (Ps 68:5). Infants certainly inherit Adam's guilt and corruption; however, if they were punished in hell, they would have no understanding of why they were being punished. R.A. Webb stated it this way:

> [If a deceased infant] were sent to hell on no other account than that of original sin, there would be a good

reason to the divine mind for the judgment, but the child's mind would be a perfect blank as to the reason of its suffering. Under such circumstances, it would know suffering, but it would have no understanding of the reason for its suffering. It could not tell its neighbor—it could not tell itself—why it was so awfully smitten; and consequently the whole meaning and significance of its sufferings, being to it a conscious enigma, the very essence of penalty would be absent, and justice would be disappointed of its vindication. Such an infant could feel that it was in hell, but it could not explain, to its own conscience, why it was there.[13]

Because of these realities, many conclude that infants, and those with severe developmental needs who are incapable of responding to the gospel, go to heaven when they die. They don't go to heaven based on any merit of their own, but because God graciously imparts his Son's righteousness to their account (2 Cor 5:21).

With that said, since Scripture never clearly addresses it, we should not be overly dogmatic about the eternal destination of infants, either way. But, certainly, there is enough in Scripture to give us a hopeful expectation that infants, young children, and others unable to respond to the gospel because of mental incapability will be with us in heaven.

Reflection

1. What stood out most in the reading and why?
2. What happens to infants when they die and what are biblical supports for your view?
3. How should we handle this doctrine when ministering to someone who has suffered the death of a young child?

4. What other questions or applications did you take from
    the reading?

Temptations to Sin

Now the serpent was more shrewd than any of the wild animals that the LORD God had made. He said to the woman, "Is it really true that God said, 'You must not eat from any tree of the orchard'?" The woman said to the serpent, "We may eat of the fruit from the trees of the orchard; but concerning the fruit of the tree that is in the middle of the orchard God said, 'You must not eat from it, and you must not touch it, or else you will die.' " The serpent said to the woman, "Surely you will not die, for God knows that when you eat from it your eyes will open and you will be like divine beings who know good and evil." When the woman saw that the tree produced fruit that was good for food, was attractive to the eye, and was desirable for making one wise, she took some of its fruit and ate it. She also gave some of it to her husband who was with her, and he ate it.
Genesis 3:1-6 (NET)

What are some common temptations to sin? First Corinthians 10:13 (NIV) says, "No temptation has overtaken you except what is common to mankind." Also, 2 Corinthians 2:11 says, "in order that Satan might not outwit us. For we are not unaware of his schemes." Being aware of common temptations is important so that we won't succumb to them and experience the consequences of our failures. With that in mind, we will consider the temptations that Adam and Eve experienced in the Garden of Eden.

Temptation to Doubt God's Word

> Now the serpent was more shrewd than any of the wild animals that the LORD God had made. He said to the woman, "Is it really true that God said, 'You must not eat from any tree of the orchard'?"
> Genesis 3:1

The serpent, who was empowered by Satan (Rev 12:9), tempted Eve when he said, "Did God really say?" He was tempting her to doubt God's Word—what she had already heard from God about not eating from the forbidden tree. If Eve doubted God's Word, she would disobey what he said. Likewise, Satan tempts us to doubt God's Word all the time: "Is God's Word really true?" "Is it really wise to wait to have sex before marriage?" "Is marriage truly only between a man and a woman?" If we begin to doubt truth, we will fall into sin and reap the consequences of it, which could affect generations after us, even as it did with Adam and Eve.

Temptation towards Legalism and Other False Teaching

> He said to the woman, "Is it really true that God said, 'You must not eat from any tree of the orchard'?"
> Genesis 3:1

When Satan asked Eve if God had said to not eat from "any tree of the orchard," he was adding to God's law. This happens in Christianity all the time. Any time we add prohibitions that aren't in Scripture, we become legalists. "Don't eat!" "Don't drink!" and "Don't touch!" are common reframes of legalism; however, when we add to God's laws, we find that there is no grace to keep those laws. If we're able to keep them through our flesh, it leads to pride and judgmentalism. If we fail, it leads to condemnation and depression. Either way, it pushes us away from God and his grace towards our own self-sufficiency. The Pharisees were legalists. They added to God's law and boasted in their keeping of these extra commands, all the while neglecting what God actually said. It created pride that pushed them away from God and others. Beware of legalism—adding to God's laws.

In fact, we should be careful of any type of false teaching, whether that be adding to God's law or taking away from it. Satan always spreads counterfeit teachings in the church to lead people away from God. Paul called them "demonic teachings" (1 Tim 4:1). We must beware of them.

Temptation to Doubt God's Goodness

> The woman said to the serpent, "We may eat of the fruit from the trees of the orchard; but concerning the fruit of the tree that is in the middle of the orchard God said, 'You must not eat from it, and you must not touch it, or else you will die.' " The serpent said to the woman, "Surely you will not die, for God knows that when you eat from it your eyes will open and you will be like divine beings who know good and evil."
> Genesis 3:2-5

After Eve corrected the serpent, saying that they could eat from every tree except one, Satan aimed to make her doubt God's goodness. He said, "Surely you will not die, for God knows that when you eat from it your eyes will open and you will be like divine beings who know good and evil" (v. 5). Essentially, Satan called God a liar and implied that he was keeping good things away from her. Satan wanted Eve to not only doubt God's Word but his goodness as well. Similarly, when Satan tested Job, his desire was to make Job curse God (Job 1:11). He wanted Job to believe that God didn't love him and have good things for him.

Satan does the same with us. He wants us to doubt God's goodness and love, so we'll ultimately turn away from God and curse him. Beware of doubts about God's love and good plans for us. In Jeremiah 29:11, God said this to Israel: "For I know what I have planned for you,' says the LORD. 'I have plans to prosper you, not to harm you. I have plans to give you a future filled with hope." No doubt, this is true for us as well. Romans 8:28 says he works all things for our good, including bad things.

Temptation towards Independence from God

> The serpent said to the woman, "Surely you will not die, for God knows that when you eat from it your eyes will open and you will be like divine beings who know good and evil."
> Genesis 3:4-5

The tree was placed in the garden to remind Adam and Eve that they were not God. Though ruling the earth, they were to do so in submission to and dependence on God. He would direct them, including telling them what was good and bad. Therefore, Satan tempted them towards independence—to not rely on God and to seek their knowledge apart from him. In the same way, we are constantly tempted towards independence. When we live apart from God's Word, prayer, and the church, we are living independently of God. In fact, we must discipline ourselves to remain dependent on God by practicing spiritual disciplines.

Paul said this to Timothy: "train yourself for godliness" or "discipline" yourself (1 Tim 5:8). Since we live independently from God by nature after Adam and Eve's rebellion, we must discipline ourselves daily to rely on God.

Be careful of living independently from God, according to our own wisdom or that of the world. We must allow God to lead and guide us. Christ taught that to enter the kingdom of heaven, we must become like a child (Matt 18:3)—dependent on the

Father for salvation—but he also taught that the "greatest in the kingdom" are like little children (Matt 18:4). To be saved, we must put our faith in Christ to deliver us from sin and its consequences, but also, to grow in our faith, we must continue to learn childlike dependence on God. In fact, the ones God has used the greatest for his kingdom have depended on him the most. Jesus is the perfect example of this childlike dependence. He always said, "I only say the words my Father says." "The works I do are from the Father." And, "I only do the Father's will." Beware of living independently of the Father—that is natural to our flesh and one of Satan's chief temptations. Christ said, without abiding in him—being totally dependent on him like a child—we can do nothing (John 15:5).

Temptation from the Flesh, the Eyes, and Pride

> When the woman saw that the tree produced fruit that was good for food, was attractive to the eye, and was desirable for making one wise, she took some of its fruit and ate it. She also gave some of it to her husband who was with her, and he ate it.
> Genesis 3:6

After Satan directed Eve towards the tree, she experienced several other temptations which are common to all people. In 1 John 2:16 (NIV), John calls them, "the lust of the flesh, the lust of the eyes, and the pride of life." When Eve saw that the fruit was "good for food," she experienced the lust of the flesh. These are any natural desires, which aren't bad in themselves, such as: eating, drinking, sleeping, and having sex. All of these desires are good when practiced properly. However, when practiced outside of God's will, they are bad and even destructive. Eating is needed to survive, but gluttony is sin. Sleeping is needed to function, but out of balance, it becomes laziness. Recreation is good to be refreshed, but it can quickly become idolatry. The desire for sex is healthy in a marriage, but outside of God's will, it can lead to pornography, adultery, rape, and even terminal disease.

When Eve saw the food was "attractive," she experienced the lust of the eyes. Proverbs 27:20 says, "As Death and Destruction are never satisfied, so the eyes of a person are never satisfied." Though Eve had every tree in the garden, she was not satisfied. She wanted more, including what God had forbidden. Likewise, we are often not satisfied with what God has given us—our friends, family, jobs, homes, cars, phones, and other amenities. Therefore, we complain and lust for what we don't have. In 1 Timothy 6:6-8, Paul said,

> Now godliness combined with contentment brings great profit. For we have brought nothing into this world and so we cannot take a single thing out either. But if we have food and shelter, we will be satisfied with that.

"Shelter," literally, means "covering" and, therefore, probably refers to shelter and clothing. We must learn to be content with godliness and the necessities of life. If God gives us more, that is great, but we shouldn't be discontent and disgruntled without it. In order to not be tempted, Eve had to be content with what God had given her. We must learn to be content as well.

Finally, Eve was tempted by the pride of life. She was not only drawn to the fruit because it was "good for food" and "attractive" to the eyes, but also because it would make her "wise" like God. The pride of being like God drew her to eat of the tree. This was the same temptation that caused Satan to fall while serving as an angel—he wanted to be like God (Is 14:13-14). Pride is often the motivator behind many of our actions, including seemingly neutral ones, such as the careers we choose, who we marry, the car we drive, and the clothing we wear. Pride also drives people to do many obviously bad things—stealing, criticizing others, and fighting. In Ecclesiastes 4:4, Solomon said it this way: "And I saw that all toil and all achievement spring from one person's envy of another. This too is meaningless, a chasing after the wind." Our pride, including coveting what others have, is an offense to God. James 4:6 says, "God opposes the proud, but he gives grace to the humble." Also, Proverbs 16:18 says, "Pride goes before destruction, and a haughty spirit before a fall." Beware of pride, it leads to further sin and disastrous consequences, including God's discipline.

Satan tempted Eve with the lust of the flesh, the lust of the eyes, and the pride of life. He does the same with us, often through the media and our peers; so we must be careful of these widespread temptations.

Temptation from Relationships, Including Societal Pressure

...She also gave some of it to her husband who was with her, and he ate it.
Genesis 3:6b

After Eve experienced all these temptations, she ate of the tree's fruit and then gave some to her husband, Adam. What's interesting about this is that Scripture says Eve was deceived and that Adam was not. In 1 Timothy 2:14, Paul said, "And Adam was not deceived, but the woman, because she was fully deceived, fell into transgression." This means that Adam sinned because his wife did—though he understood the morality and consequences of her decision. He experienced a form of "peer pressure." We can be sure that was Satan's original plan. As taught previously, since Adam was the federal head of creation, his sin would affect not only himself, but all of creation, including all humans. Adam and Eve were co-rulers of creation, but God made Adam her head (cf. Gen 2:23, 3:20, 1 Cor 11:3, Rom 5:12-14). Therefore, Satan's ultimate goal was probably to use Eve to get Adam to sin. Likewise, Satan commonly does the same with us. He will use friends, family, co-workers, and society in general to press us to rebel against God. First Corinthians 15:33 says, "Do not be deceived: 'Bad company corrupts good morals.'" Proverbs 13:20 says, "… a companion of fools suffers harm." Satan aims to lead us into destruction through temptations from our associations, including the pressure of the world—an evil system which he controls. Since Satan rules the world (cf. John 14:30), there will always be great societal and cultural pressures on believers that don't align with God's Word. Romans 12:2 says, "Do not be conformed to this present world, but be transformed by the renewing of your mind."

Though relationships can be some of the biggest catalysts for spiritual growth and obeying God, Satan commonly tries to use them for evil. We must decide to follow God, even if everybody else turns away. Also, we must realize that even godly people and people we love can, at times, be used by the enemy to tempt us to sin. Job had to rebuke his wife who encouraged him to curse God and die (Job 2:9). Christ had to rebuke Satan who spoke through his chief disciple, Peter—encouraging him to avoid the cross (Matt 16:23). We must wisely discern the voice of Satan through others, even as Job and Christ did. The primary way we do this is by knowing God's Word so well that we can easily discern lies, regardless of who they come through. To avoid temptation, we must be careful when Satan brings it through others. This is often the most powerful kind of temptation.

Conclusion

What are common temptations towards sin that people experience?

1. Temptation to Doubt God's Word
2. Temptation towards Legalism and Other False Teaching
3. Temptation to Doubt God's Goodness
4. Temptation towards Independence from God

5. Temptation from the Flesh, the Eyes, and Pride
6. Temptation from Relationships, Including Societal Pressure

Reflection

1. Which temptation(s) stood out most and why?
2. Why is being aware of common temptations so important for conquering temptation (1 Cor 10:13, 2 Cor 2:11)?
3. What are some other practices or insights that are helpful with conquering temptation?
4. What other questions or applications did you take from the reading?

Consequences of Sin

When the woman saw that the tree produced fruit that was good for food, was attractive to the eye, and was desirable for making one wise, she took some of its fruit and ate it. She also gave some of it to her husband who was with her, and he ate it. Then the eyes of both of them opened, and they knew they were naked; so they sewed fig leaves together and made coverings for themselves. Then the man and his wife heard the sound of the LORD God moving about in the orchard at the breezy time of the day, and they hid from the LORD God among the trees of the orchard. But the LORD God called to the man and said to him, "Where are you?" The man replied, "I heard you moving about in the orchard, and I was afraid because I was naked, so I hid." And the LORD God said, "Who told you that you were naked? Did you eat from the tree that I commanded you not to eat from?" The man said, "The woman whom you gave me, she gave me some fruit from the tree and I ate it." So the LORD God said to the woman, "What is this you have done?" And the woman replied, "The serpent tricked me, and I ate." The LORD God said to the serpent, "Because you have done this, cursed are you above all the wild beasts and all the living creatures of the field! On your belly you will crawl and dust you will eat all the days of your life. And I will put hostility between you and the woman and between your offspring and her offspring; her offspring will attack your head, and you will attack her offspring's heel." To the woman he said, "I will

greatly increase your labor pains; with pain you will give birth to children. You will want to control your husband, but he will dominate you." But to Adam he said, "Because you obeyed your wife and ate from the tree about which I commanded you, 'You must not eat from it,' cursed is the ground thanks to you; in painful toil you will eat of it all the days of your life. It will produce thorns and thistles for you, but you will eat the grain of the field. By the sweat of your brow you will eat food until you return to the ground, for out of it you were taken; for you are dust, and to dust you will return."
Genesis 3:6-19 (NET)

What are the consequences of sin? We've considered some of them throughout our study, such as humanity experiencing Adam's guilt and therefore death (Rom 5:12, 17), and also humanity receiving Adam's sin nature (Psalm 51:5, Gal 5:17-20)—a propensity to sin; however, these consequences and more were first introduced by God after the fall.

Right after Adam and Eve's sin in the garden, God prophesied numerous, severe consequences from their failure, which would affect not only them but also their children and all of creation. Many of these consequences get worse as people continue to practice sin. As we study these, it shows us why the world is the way it is, but it also warns us against continuing in our parents' disregard for God and his Word.

Humanity Has the Capacity to Do Great Evil

When the woman saw that the tree produced fruit that was good for food, was attractive to the eye, and was desirable for making one wise, she took some of its fruit and ate it. She also gave some of it to her husband who was with her, and he ate it. Then the eyes of both of them

opened, and they knew they were naked; so they sewed fig leaves together and made coverings for themselves.
Genesis 3:6-7

When Adam and Eve ate of the tree of the knowledge of good and evil (3:6), immediately their eyes were "opened," and they knew they were naked (v. 7). The tree of the knowledge of good and evil gave them knowledge to do both great good and great evil (Gen 2:17). Humans have the capacity to create wonderful architecture, artwork, and make great discoveries in science, including cures for diseases. But, they also have the capacity to create great evil, including harmful drugs and weapons of mass destruction. Before the fall, humans only had the capacity to do great good, and only by depending upon God. But now, both good and evil can be done independent of God. In fact, "good" can even be done in defiance of God. For example, all the good works the Pharisees did—their giving, fasting, and teaching—were done to bring glory to themselves, as they sought the praise and affection of people instead of God (cf. Matt 6:1-5). Humanity's good works are the same—when done apart from God, they are just a veil for vanity or an effort to achieve some self-oriented benefit, including salvation. Therefore, even humanity's so called "good works" are evil to God. Isaiah 64:6 says, "We are all like one who is unclean, all our so-called righteous acts are like a menstrual rag in your sight."
Because of the fall, humanity has a sin nature and a tremendous capacity to do great evil. Galatians 5:19-21 describes the works of the flesh, which are innate, within every person:

Now the works of the flesh are obvious: sexual immorality, impurity, depravity, idolatry, sorcery, hostilities, strife, jealousy, outbursts of anger, selfish rivalries, dissensions, factions, envying, murder, drunkenness, carousing, and similar things. I am warning you, as I had warned you before: Those who practice such things will not inherit the kingdom of God!

Some of these works seem mundane, like "envying," while others are tremendously evil, like "murder" and "sexual immorality," which include things like suicide, manslaughter, genocide, adultery, homosexuality, pedophilia, and rape. However, it must be realized that all of these are inside every person because we all have a flesh. Some are more prone to certain sins because of family history, abuse, or other types of exposure. Because of our parents' eating of the forbidden tree, we now have a flesh and a tremendous capacity for evil.

Humanity Lacks Transparency and Intimacy with One Another

> ... they knew they were naked; so they sewed fig leaves together and made coverings for themselves.
> Genesis 3:6

When Adam and Eve knew they were naked, they hid from one another and clothed themselves with fig leaves. Previously, Adam and Eve lived in a perfectly transparent relationship with no secrets, but after the fall, that was lost. Likewise, today, people struggle with transparency. They live in fear of what people will think or say about them; therefore, they hide in shame—keeping secrets from one another. Even families often don't share everything with one another. Shame is also a more dominant characteristic in certain cultures and with certain individuals. This is a result of the fall. Because of fear and shame, people lack transparency and therefore the genuine intimate relationships with one another we are meant to have.

Humanity Lacks Transparency and Intimacy with God

> Then the man and his wife heard the sound of the LORD God moving about in the orchard at the breezy time of the day, and they hid from the LORD God among the trees of the orchard.
> Genesis 3:8

When Adam and Eve heard God walking in the garden, they hid from him. As mentioned previously, Adam and Eve died, in a sense, immediately after they ate from the tree. Death simply means separation. After the fall, Adam and Eve were separated from God. They began to hide from him because of their sin, and so do humans today. Scripture is not the story of people seeking God; it is the story of God seeking after people who have turned away from God. Isaiah 53:6 says, "All of us had wandered off like sheep; each of us had strayed off on his own path." Also, Romans 3:11 says, "No one seeks God." Certainly, people go on spiritual journeys where they attempt to seek God, but their natures, apart from God's grace, don't seek the true God. Instead, they seek, create, and worship idols. Romans 1:22-23 says, "Although they claimed to be wise, they became fools and exchanged the glory of the immortal God for an image resembling mortal human beings or birds or four-footed animals or reptiles." Humans, because of their sin natures, are idol factories. Apart from God's grace removing their blindness (2 Cor 4:4-6), they create and worship gods of their imagination instead of the true God. In fact, Romans 8:7 says "the outlook of the flesh is hostile to God, for it does not submit to the law of God, nor is it able to do so." Our flesh, referring to our sinful nature, is hostile to God, won't submit to him, and can't do so. First Corinthians 2:14 says, "The unbeliever does not receive the things of the Spirit of God, for they are foolishness to him. And he cannot understand them, because they are spiritually discerned." People don't seek God, can't understand him, and won't submit to him. Adam's rebellious nature was passed on to his seed, which is why we need God to seek us, to draw us to himself (John 6:44), and even give us faith to be saved (Eph 2:8-9, Phil 1:29). At the fall, people lost intimacy and transparency with God. Instead, they hide from God, suppress the truth of his existence and righteous nature, and worship false gods, including themselves (Rom 1:18-22).

Humanity Struggles with Fear

> But the LORD God called to the man and said to him, "Where are you?" The man replied, "I heard you moving about in the orchard, and I was afraid because I was naked, so I hid."
> Genesis 3:9-10

After the fall, Adam experienced a new emotion, which was fear. Before the fall, Adam and Eve had never been afraid. First John 4:18 says, "perfect love drives out fear." Since they dwelled in perfect, loving relationships with God and one another, they never struggled with fear. However, when sin entered the world, humans, by nature, rejected God's perfect love and became incapable of perfectly loving one another; therefore, fear became the norm. They would fear God, one another, the future, the past, disaster, animals, and many other things. Certainly, this all is true today. People live in fear. Fear is actually what drives the insurance industry. People are afraid of getting into a car accident or experiencing natural disasters like hurricanes and tornadoes. They are afraid of dying. Sometimes, they are afraid of living too long and getting old. People are afraid. In fact, since God did not make humans to live in fear, it has devastating effects on our mind and body. When we are living in anxiety and fear, it often causes our bodies to turn on themselves; we start to struggle with sickness and depression, which come from fear and stress (cf. Prov 12:25, 17:22). As happened with Adam, fear also can make us irrational. Because of these irrational fears, we at times even turn away from those who love us most, like God, friends, and family, and at worst, even seek to hurt them. Because of the fall, people struggle with many phobias.

Humanity Blames Others Instead of Accepting Personal Responsibility

> And the LORD God said, "Who told you that you were naked? Did you eat from the tree that I commanded you not to eat from?" The man said, "The woman whom you gave me, she gave me some fruit from the tree and I ate it." So the LORD God said to the woman, "What is this you have done?" And the woman replied, "The serpent tricked me, and I ate."
> Genesis 3:11-13

When God asked Adam if he ate from the tree, he didn't simply answer, "Yes." He blamed the woman and by implication, God. He said, "The woman whom YOU gave me, she gave me some fruit from the tree and I ate it" (emphasis added). Then, God asked the woman, who also didn't simply accept responsibility; she blamed the serpent. And this is now a normal characteristic of our sinful nature—avoiding responsibility and blaming others. Instead of accepting personal responsibility, people blame their parents, the school system, the government, God, Satan, and even sin itself. Commonly, especially in psychological circles, sin is looked at as a disease or orientation, instead of as one's personal choice. For the drunk who beats his wife, he is at times told, "It's not your fault! You have a disease!" However, unless people accept personal responsibility for their sin, they will never be set free from it. This is now the nature of humanity—avoiding or lessening responsibility by blaming others.

Humanity, and Specifically Women, Are in a Cosmic Battle with Evil Forces

> The LORD God said to the serpent, "Because you have done this, cursed are you above all the wild beasts and all the living creatures of the field! On your belly you will crawl and dust you will eat all the days of your life. And I will put hostility between you and the woman…
> Genesis 3:14-15

After Adam and Eve accepted responsibility, God cursed the serpent and declared that he would slither on the ground all the days of his life (v. 14). Also, God declared that there would be enmity between the serpent and the woman (v. 15). These prophecies seem to have dual fulfillments. Apparently, snakes initially walked instead of slithering on the ground. God held the snake culpable for submitting to Satan (cf. Rev 12:9). But, the prophecy also was spoken to the spirit empowering the serpent, Satan. There would be an enduring enmity between the serpent and the woman.

How is the enmity between the serpent and the woman seen? No doubt, it is, in part, seen in the troubled history women have had. They have often been enslaved, trafficked, and sexually abused. They have also experienced a continual fight for equal rights with men—the right to vote, to have equal wages, and job opportunities. This fight, though having led to many good things, has also at times led to many evils, including women neglecting their call to be a wife and mother, as though these callings are oppressive. It has also led many to abort their children and champion abortion as a woman's right. This enmity between Satan and the woman is also seen in how women's bodies are often exploited. They are used to sell every product under the sun—cologne, beer, food, cars, and houses. This exploitation often creates great insecurities in women. They have to have the perfect body, skin, and smile. These insecurities often lead to all types of disorders—anxiety disorder, depressive disorder, and eating disorder, among others. It does not take much consideration of society to see how there is a great enmity between Satan and the woman.

Though the prophecy is focused on the enmity between Satan and the woman, it certainly includes, to some extent, all who would come from her—males and females. Satan and his demons are in a continual battle to steal, kill, and destroy people (cf. John 10:10)—keeping them away from God and their God-ordained callings. Satan and his demons are against all people, but they have a special enmity against women.

Humanity Is Antagonistic to Christ (and His Followers)

> And I will put hostility between you and the woman and between your offspring and her offspring; her offspring will attack your head, and you will attack her offspring's heel."
> Genesis 3:15

When God spoke about Satan's enmity against the woman's offspring, he had one particular male offspring in mind—Christ who would eventually defeat Satan. Genesis 3:15 is often called the proto-gospel—the first gospel. Satan would attack the heel of Christ, a flesh wound, and Christ would attack Satan's head—a mortal blow. This ultimately happened at the cross. When Christ died, it seemed like a victory for Satan, but it was short-lived. Ultimately, in the resurrection, Christ defeated the devil, and one day Christ will destroy all the works of the devil by restoring creation. First John 3:8 says, "...For this purpose the Son of God was revealed: to destroy the works of the devil."

Another aspect of this prophecy is how Satan's offspring would have enmity with the messiah. Who is the offspring of Satan? Scripture actually says that everybody is born an offspring of Satan until they are born again into the family of God (cf. John 3:1-8). First John 3:10 says, "By this the children of God and the children of the devil are revealed: Everyone who does not practice righteousness—the one who does not love his fellow Christian—is not of God." Therefore, humanity has a natural enmity towards Christ, which was demonstrated when Israel and the Romans crucified him. In John 8:40-44, Jesus actually told the Pharisees that they were doing the deeds of their father, the devil, by trying to kill him. Their father was a murderer and so were they, as they eventually succeeded in killing him. This enmity was also seen in how the early church was persecuted for their belief in Christ—leading the church to spread throughout the ancient world (Acts 8:1, 11:19-20). Likewise, persecution towards believers has only increased since then. Jesus taught that in the end times his disciples would be hated by all nations for his name's sake (Matt 24:9). History has born this out. There were more martyrs in this last century than all the previous centuries combined. Today, some statistics say that around 246 believers are martyred every day. [14] Certainly, God's original prophecy about enmity towards the promised seed has been fulfilled over and over again. The enmity towards Christ and his followers continues to grow, and no doubt, Christ's prophecy will fully come true. Believers will be hated by every nation because of his name's sake (Matt 24:9).

Humanity, and Specifically Women, Experience Great Pains in Childbirth

> To the woman he said, "I will greatly increase your labor pains; with pain you will give birth to children...
> Genesis 3:16

When God described the woman's pain in childbirth, this seems to refer to more than birth contractions. The woman would experience pain in the death of the child and sometimes her death from labor. There would be pain, at times, in not being able to bear children. There are many pains associated with childbearing.

In addition, it appears that these pains are still increasingly experienced when God judges a society because of their unrestrained sin. Consider what God said to Israel in Hosea 9:11-14:

> Ephraim will be like a bird; what they value will fly away. They will not bear children— they will not enjoy pregnancy— they will not even conceive! Even if they raise their children, I will take away every last one of them. Woe to them! For I will turn away from them. Just as lion cubs are born predators, so Ephraim will bear his sons for slaughter. Give them, O LORD—what will you give them? Give them wombs that miscarry, and breasts that cannot nurse!

Because of Israel's sin, they would struggle with getting pregnant (v. 11). When they did get pregnant, their children would be taken away from them (v. 12). Some would die in the womb from miscarriages; others would die after birth for various reasons. Hosea said they would bear sons for the "slaughter" (v. 13)—possibly as they die by accidents, street violence, or war.

No doubt, many of our societies are experiencing these same judgments because of our individual and national sins—difficulty in having children and the early death of children. Many of these premature deaths are at the hands of parents, doctors, and governments through abortions. Scripture teaches that pain in childbearing is a result of the fall, but it also increases because of individual and corporate sin.

Humanity Experiences Great Discord within Marriage (and Other Relationships)

> You will want to control your husband, but he will dominate you.
> Genesis 3:16b

God also told Eve that she would experience great discord within her marriage. Before the fall, there was perfect bliss in the marriage. The husband would love his wife, and the wife would respect and follow her husband (cf. Eph 5:22-33). However, after the fall, everything was switched. The wife, instead of submitting to her husband, would try to control him. She would often do this through manipulation—using sex. Or sometimes through her constant complaining. Solomon described how a nagging wife was like a constant dripping (Prov 27:15). He said it was better to live on a corner of the housetop than in a house with a quarrelsome wife (Prov 21:9). However, the curse doesn't stop there; it also affected the husband. Instead of gently leading his wife, the husband would seek to dominate her. He would do this through his harsh words and sometimes through physical abuse, including sexual abuse. Because of sin, couples experience the battle of the sexes, instead of the joy of perfectly complementing each other, as God originally planned. In various societies, we see extremes on both ends. In some, the husband is the doormat—the wife makes all the decisions and rules the home. In others, the wife is the doormat—she is to be unseen and unheard.

This curse is even seen outside of marriage, amongst singles. It is seen in the predatorial woman who uses her beauty and manipulation to control men—making her way up the corporate ladder, or by luring financially successful men into relationships, or simply through prostitution. We also see this in the predatorial man who tries to conquer and sleep with as many women as possible—treating them as prey, instead of as humans with dignity and honor.

With all that said, this discord between husbands and wives is simply a picture of what would happen throughout society. There would be discord among siblings, co-workers, political parties, ethnic groups, and nations. Because of conflict, society experiences very little peace. Since the foundation of society—the home—is broken, every other facet of society is broken as well. This is all a result of the fall.

Humanity Experiences the Curse throughout the Earth

But to Adam he said, "Because you obeyed your wife and ate from the tree about which I commanded you, 'You must not eat from it,' cursed is the ground thanks to you … It will produce thorns and thistles for you, but you will eat the grain of the field.
Genesis 3:17a, 18

Since Adam was originally placed as head over creation, his fall affected all of creation negatively. God cursed the ground (v. 17); instead of being fruitful, it would produce thorns and thistles (v. 18). Romans 8:20 says creation was subjected to "frustration" (NIV) because of Adam's sin. These frustrations are seen in famines where there is no food, droughts with no water, earthquakes, typhoons, volcanic eruptions, and the like. Because of Adam's sin, creation was cursed.

In fact, like with women's childbearing, the earth is still affected by humanity's continual sin. In Genesis 4, because Cain killed his brother, God made Cain a wanderer. He would be a wanderer because wherever he went, the ground would not consistently produce crops. Therefore, he would have to wander to eat. In Genesis 4:11-12, God said this to Cain:

So now, you are banished from the ground, which has opened its mouth to receive your brother's blood from your hand. When you try to cultivate the ground it will no longer yield its best for you. You will be a homeless wanderer on the earth.

Also, when the world became corrupt in Genesis 7, God brought the flood, which destroyed all of mankind, except Noah's family. Likewise, with Israel, God commanded them to not practice the sins of the Canaanites lest they defile the land and it vomit them up (Lev 18:27-28). Throughout Israel's history, there were famines and droughts, sometimes for years (1 Kings 17-18), because of their rebellion against God. Our sins still affect the land negatively. In fact, Christ said that in the last days, humanity's sin would be so bad, the land would react as if it were in birth pains. There will be great earthquakes, famines, pestilence, and cosmic disasters (Matt 24:7-8, 29).

Humanity Experiences the Curse, including Pain and Frustration, in Work

> in painful toil you will eat of it all the days of your life. It will produce thorns and thistles for you, but you will eat the grain of the field. By the sweat of your brow you will eat food
> Genesis 3:17b-19a

When Adam worked, he would experience "painful toil" (v. 17) and "sweat" (v. 19). In addition, his work would not always produce the expected outcome. Sometimes, instead of producing fruit, it produced "thorns and thistles" (v. 18)—creating great frustration. It must be remembered that God originally gave Adam and Eve work before the fall. They were to not only fill the earth but "subdue it" and "rule" over it (Gen 1:28). This means they were to be good stewards of the earth—studying it, mining its resources, using it to feed themselves and others, and helping it prosper. Work was meant to be a blessing and a way to imitate God who worked by creating the earth and who works in maintaining it (Col 1:17, Matt 6:26-30). However, after the fall, humanity would experience pain and frustration in work. This has been true throughout history. Though work is a great joy and the way we provide for ourselves, it is a constant pain and source of frustration. Studies show that most people are unsatisfied with their work and many hate it.[15] No doubt, because of this reality, Solomon realized that when people find enjoyment in their labor, it is a gift from God. In Ecclesiastes 2:24, he said, "There is nothing better for people than to eat and drink, and to find enjoyment in their work. I also perceived that this ability to find enjoyment comes from God." As a result of the curse, people struggle with great pain and frustration in their work, instead of the enjoyment and fruitfulness God originally intended.

Humanity Ultimately Experiences Death

> By the sweat of your brow you will eat food until you return to the ground, for out of it you were taken; for you are dust, and to dust you will return."
> Genesis 3:19

Finally, God told Adam that he would die, which was a fulfillment of God's original warning to not eat of the forbidden tree lest they die (Gen 2:17). Death was going to happen to Adam and Eve and their children. When we get to Genesis 5, we find the first genealogy, which essentially repeatedly says, "So and so lived and then he died, so and so lived and then he died..." (paraphrase). Now, every person will die. Hebrews 9:27 says, "... people are appointed to die once, and then to face judgment."

It should be noted that in Genesis 3:22, God says this about Adam: "he must not be allowed to stretch out his hand and take also from the tree of life and eat, and live forever." God did not want people to live in this sinful condition forever; therefore, they were not allowed to eat of the tree of life. In that sense, death is a blessing, specifically for those who give their lives to Christ (John 3:16). One day, at death, God will free believers from our sinful nature and the consequences of it. And when Christ returns, he will resurrect believers, heal the land, and restore God's creation (cf. Col 1:19-20, Rev 20, Rev 21:1). Until then, we must put our hope in Christ and follow him.

Conclusion

What are the consequences of sin, and thus the fall?

1. Humanity Has the Capacity to Do Great Evil
2. Humanity Lacks Transparency and Intimacy with One Another
3. Humanity Lacks Transparency and Intimacy with God
4. Humanity Struggles with Fear
5. Humanity Blames Others Instead of Accepting Personal Responsibility
6. Humanity, and Specifically Women, Are in a Cosmic Battle with Evil Forces
7. Humanity Is Antagonistic to Christ (and His Followers)
8. Humanity, and Specifically Women, Experience Great Pains in Childbirth
9. Humanity Experiences Great Discord within Marriage (and Other Relationships)
10. Humanity Experiences the Curse throughout the Earth
11. Humanity Experiences the Curse, including Pain and Frustration, in Work
12. Humanity, Ultimately, Experiences Death

Reflection

1. Which consequence(s) of the fall stood out most and why?
2. In what ways do we see the enmity between Satan and the woman in society?

3. How does humanity's continual practice of sin increase the experience of many of these consequences in society? Give examples.
4. What other questions or applications did you take from the reading?

Study Group Tips

Leading a small group using the Bible Teacher's Guide can be done in various ways. One format for leading a small group is the "study group" model, where each member prepares and shares in the teaching. This appendix will cover tips for facilitating a weekly study group.

1. Each week the members of the study group will read through a selected chapter of the guide, answer the reflection questions (see Appendix 2), and come prepared to share with the group.

2. Prior to each meeting, a different member can be chosen to lead the group and share Question 1 of the reflection questions, which is to give a short summary of the chapter read. This section of the gathering could last from five to fifteen minutes. This way, each member can develop their gift of teaching. It also will make them study harder during the week. Or, each week the same person could share the summary.

3. After the summary has been given, the leader for that week will facilitate discussions through the rest of the reflection questions and also ask select review questions from the chapter.

4. After discussion, the group will share prayer requests and pray for one another.

The strength of the study group is the fact that the members will be required to prepare their responses before the meeting, which will allow for easier discussion. In addition, each member will be given the opportunity to teach, which will further equip their ministry skills. The study group model has distinct advantages.

Reflection Questions

Writing is one of the best ways to learn. In class, we take notes and write papers, and these methods are used to help us learn and retain the material. The same is true with the Word of God. Obviously, all the authors of Scripture were writers. This helped them better learn the Scriptures and also enabled them to more effectively teach it. As you reflect on God's Word, using the Bible Teacher's Guide, take time to write so you can similarly grow both in your learning and teaching.

1. How would you summarize the main points of the text/chapter? Write a brief summary.

2. What stood out to you most in the reading? Did any of the contents trigger any memories or experiences? If so, please share them.

3. What follow–up questions did you have about the reading? What parts did you not fully agree with?

4. What applications did you take from the reading, and how do you plan to implement them into your life?

5. Write several commitment statements: As a result of my time studying God's Word, I will . . .

6. What are some practical ways to pray as a result of studying the text? Spend some time ministering to the Lord through prayer.

Walking the Romans Road

How can a person be saved? From what is he saved? How can someone have eternal life? Scripture teaches that, after death, each person will spend eternity either in heaven or hell. How can a person go to heaven?

Paul said this to Timothy:

> You, however, must continue in the things you have learned and are confident about. You know who taught you and how from infancy you have known the holy writings, which are able to give you wisdom for salvation through faith in Christ Jesus.
> 2 Timothy 3:14-15

One of the reasons God gave us Scripture is to make us wise for salvation. This means that without it, nobody can know how to be saved.

Well then, how can a people be saved and what are they being saved from? A common method of sharing the good news of salvation is through the Romans Road. One of the great themes, not only of the Bible, but specifically of the book of Romans, is salvation. In Romans, the author, Paul, clearly details the steps we must take in order to be saved.

How can we be saved? What steps must we take?

Step One: We Must Accept that We Are Sinners

Romans 3:23 says, "For all have sinned and fall short of the glory of God." What does it mean to sin? The word sin means "to miss the mark." The mark we missed is reflecting God's image. When God created mankind in the Genesis narrative, he created man in the "image of God" (1:27). The "image of God" means many things, but most importantly it means we were made to be holy just as he is holy. Man was made moral. We were meant to reflect God's holiness in every way: the way we think, the way we talk, and the way we act. And any time we miss the mark in these areas, we commit sin.

Furthermore, we do not only sin when we commit a sinful act, such as lying, stealing, or cheating. We sin anytime we have a wrong heart motive. The greatest commandments in Scripture are to "Love the Lord your God with all your heart and to love your neighbor as yourself" (Matt 22:36-40, paraphrase). Whenever we don't love God supremely and love others as ourselves, we sin and fall short of the glory of God. For this reason, man is always in a state of sinning. Sadly, even if our actions are good, our heart is bad. I have never loved God with my whole heart, mind, and soul, and neither has anybody else. Therefore, we have all sinned and fall short of the glory of God (Rom 3:23). We have all missed the mark of God's holiness and we must accept this.

What's the next step?

Step Two: We Must Understand We Are Under the Judgment of God

Why are we under the judgment of God? It is because of our sins. Scripture teaches that God is not only a loving God, but he is also a just God. And his justice requires judgment for each of our sins. Romans 6:23 says, "For the payoff of sin is death."

A payoff or wage is something we earn. Every time we sin, we earn the wage of death. What is death? Death really means separation. In physical death, the body is separated from the spirit, but in spiritual death, man is separated from God. Man currently lives in a state of spiritual death (cf. Eph 2:1-3). We do not love God, obey him, or know him as we should. Therefore, man is in a state of death.

Moreover, on the day of our physical death, if we have not been saved, we will spend eternity separated from God in a very real hell. In hell, we will pay the wage for each of our sins. Therefore, in hell people will experience various degrees of punishment (cf. Lk 12:47-48). This places man in a very dangerous predicament—unholy and therefore under the judgment of God.

How should we respond to this? This leads us to our third step.

Step Three: We Must Recognize God Has Invited All to Accept His Free Gift of Salvation

Romans 6:23 does not stop at the wages of sin being death. It says, "For the payoff of sin is death, but the gift of God is eternal life in Christ Jesus our Lord." Because God loved everybody on the earth, he offered the free gift of eternal life, which anyone can receive through Jesus Christ.

Because it is a gift, it cannot be earned. We cannot work for it. Ephesians 2:8-9 says, "For by grace you are saved through faith, and this is not from yourselves, it is the gift of God; it is not from works, so that no one can boast."

Going to church, being baptized, giving to the poor, or doing any other righteous work does not save. Salvation is a gift that must be received from God. It is a gift that has been prepared by his effort alone.

How do we receive this free gift?

Step Four: We Must Believe Jesus Christ Died for Our Sins and Rose from the Dead

If we are going to receive this free gift, we must believe in God's Son, Jesus Christ. Because God loved us, cared for us, and didn't want us to be separated from him eternally, he sent his Son to die for our sins. Romans 5:8 says, "But God demonstrates his own love for us, in that while we were still sinners, Christ died for us." Similarly, John 3:16 says, "For this is the way God loved the world: He gave his one and only Son, so that everyone who believes in him will not perish but have eternal life." God so loved us that he gave his only Son for our sins.

Jesus Christ was a real, historical person who lived 2,000 years ago. He was born of a virgin. He lived a perfect life. He was put to death by the Romans and the Jews. And after he was buried, he rose again on the third day. In his death, he took our sins and God's wrath for those sins and gave us his perfect righteousness so we could be accepted by God. Second Corinthians 5:21 says, "God made the one who did not know sin to be sin for us, so that in him we would become the righteousness of God." God did all this so we could be saved from his wrath.

Christ's death satisfied the just anger of God over our sins. When God looked at Jesus on the cross, he saw us and our sins and therefore judged Jesus. And now, when God sees those of us who are saved, he sees his righteous Son and accepts us. In salvation, we have become the righteousness of God.

If we are going to be saved, if we are going to receive this free gift of salvation, we must believe in Christ's death, burial, and resurrection for our sins (cf. 1 Cor 15:3-5, Rom 10:9-10). Do you believe?

Step Five: We Must Confess Christ as Lord of Our Lives

Romans 10:9-10 says,

<blockquote>

Because if you confess with your mouth that Jesus is Lord and believe in your heart that God raised him from the dead, you will be saved. For with the heart one believes and thus has righteousness and with the mouth one confesses and thus has salvation.

</blockquote>

Not only must we believe, but we must confess Christ as Lord of our lives. It is one thing to believe in Christ but another to follow Christ. Simple belief does not save. Christ must be our Lord. James said this: "…Even the demons believe that – and tremble with fear" (James 2:19), but the demons are not saved—Christ is not their Lord.

Another aspect of making Christ Lord is repentance. Repentance really means a change of mind that leads to a change of direction. Before we met Christ, we were living our own life and following our own sinful desires. But when we get saved, our mind and direction change. We start to follow Christ as Lord.

How do we make this commitment to the lordship of Christ so we can be saved? Paul said we must confess with our mouth "Jesus is Lord" as we believe in him. Romans 10:13 says, "For everyone who calls on the name of the Lord will be saved."

If you admit that you are a sinner and understand you are under God's wrath because of it; if you believe Jesus Christ is the Son of God, that he died on the cross for your sins, and rose from the dead for your salvation; if you are ready to turn from your sin and cling to Christ as Lord, you can be saved.

If this is your heart, then you can pray this prayer and commit to following Christ as your Lord.

<blockquote>

Dear heavenly Father, I confess I am a sinner and have fallen short of your glory, what you made me for. I believe Jesus Christ died on the cross to pay the penalty for my

</blockquote>

sins and rose from the dead so I can have eternal life. I am turning away from my sin and accepting you as my Lord and Savior. Come into my life and change me. Thank you for your gift of salvation.

Scripture teaches that if you truly accept Christ as your Lord, then you are a new creation. Second Corinthians 5:17 says, "So then, if anyone is in Christ, he is a new creation; what is old has passed away – look, what is new has come!" God has forgiven your sins (1 John 1:9), he has given you his Holy Spirit (Rom 8:15), and he is going to disciple you and make you into the image of his Son (cf. Rom 8:29). He will never leave you nor forsake you (Heb 13:5), and he will complete the work he has begun in your life (Phil 1:6). In heaven, angels and saints are rejoicing because of your commitment to Christ (Lk 15:7).

Praise God for his great salvation! May God keep you in his hand, empower you through the Holy Spirit, train you through mature believers, and use you to build his kingdom! "He who calls you is trustworthy, and he will in fact do this" (1 Thess 5:24). God bless you!

Coming Soon

Praise the Lord for your interest in studying and teaching God's Word. If God has blessed you through the BTG series, please partner with us in petitioning God to greatly use this series to encourage and build his Church. Also, please consider leaving an Amazon review and signing up for free book promotions. By doing this, you help spread the "Word." Thanks for your partnership in the gospel from the first day until now (Phil 1:4-5).

Available:
First Peter
Theology Proper
Building Foundations for a Godly Marriage
Colossians
God's Battle Plan for Purity
Nehemiah
Philippians
The Perfections of God
The Armor of God
Ephesians
Abraham
Finding a Godly Mate
1 Timothy
The Beatitudes
Equipping Small Group Leaders
2 Timothy
Jacob

About the Author

Greg Brown earned his MA in religion and MA in teaching from Trinity International University, a MRE from Liberty University, and a PhD in theology from Louisiana Baptist University. He has served over sixteen years in pastoral ministry and currently serves as a chaplain and professor at Handong Global University, teaching pastor at Handong International Congregation, and as a Navy Reserve chaplain.

Greg married his lovely wife, Tara Jayne, in 2006, and they have one daughter, Saiyah Grace. He enjoys going on dates with his wife, playing with his daughter, reading, writing, studying in coffee shops, working out, and following the NBA and UFC. His pursuit in life, simply stated, is "to know God and to be found faithful by Him."

To connect with Greg, please follow at http://www.pgregbrown.com.

Notes

1 Grudem, W. A. (2004). Systematic theology: an introduction to biblical doctrine (p. 490). Leicester, England; Grand Rapids, MI: Inter-Varsity Press; Zondervan Pub. House.

2 Evans, Tony. Theology You Can Count On: Experiencing What the Bible Says About... God the Father, God the Son, God the Holy Spirit, Angels, Salvation... . Moody Publishers. Kindle Edition.

3 Ryrie, C. C. (1999). Basic Theology: A Popular Systematic Guide to Understanding Biblical Truth (pp. 238–239). Chicago, IL: Moody Press.

4 Grudem, W. A. (2004). Systematic theology: an introduction to biblical doctrine (pp. 495–496). Leicester, England; Grand Rapids, MI: Inter-Varsity Press; Zondervan Pub. House.

5 Aaron, Daryl. Understanding Theology in 15 Minutes a Day: How can I know God? Baker Publishing Group. Kindle Edition.

6 Sproul, R. C. (2014). Everyone's a Theologian: An Introduction to Systematic Theology (p. 108). Orlando, FL: Reformation Trust.

7 Grudem, W. A. (2004). Systematic theology: an introduction to biblical doctrine (p. 504). Leicester, England; Grand Rapids, MI: Inter-Varsity Press; Zondervan Pub. House.

8 Accessed 8/13/20 from https://www.gotquestions.org/two-natures.html

9 MacArthur, J. (2007). 1, 2, 3 John (p. 39). Chicago, IL: Moody Publishers.

10 Guzik, D. (2013). 1 John (1 Jn 1:8–10). Santa Barbara, CA: David Guzik.

11 MacArthur, J. F., Jr. (1985). Matthew (Vol. 3, p. 179). Chicago: Moody Press.

12 MacArthur, J. F., Jr. (1985). Matthew (Vol. 3, p. 181). Chicago: Moody Press.

13 Accessed 8/11/20 from https://www.thegospelcoalition.org/article/do-all-infants-go-to-heaven/

14 Accessed 7/27/20 from https://www.foxnews.com/politics/christian-persecution-how-many-are-being-killed-where-they-are-being-killed

[15] Accessed 4/7/20 from https://www.forbes.com/sites/susanadams/2014/06/20/most-americans-are-unhappy-at-work/#4e01599341a1